To my three: Owen, Adelyn and Annamarie. I am so lucky to be your mom.

Acknowledgments

Thank you to wildlife hospitals and raptor centers everywhere. The work that you do is vital. I hope this book helps to further your efforts to educate and preserve.

Special thanks to Amanda Nicholson and the Wildlife Center of Virginia for sharing knowledge, photos and the story of Maggie; the Virginia Department of Game and Inland Fisheries for maintaining the nest cam and for sharing photos; Chad and Chris Saladin for their amazing photos from C&C's Ohio Peregrine Page (Facebook) and the Medina Raptor Center for the good work that you do; Scott Turnmeyer for sharing your beautiful pictures; the "Rfalconcam.com" for the adorable shots of young falcons and the Genesee Valley Audubon Society for giving permission to use their webcam photos; and the Raptor Center at the University of Minnesota for getting me started and for your ongoing support and enthusiasm.

Photo Credits by Photographer and Page Number

All images copyright of their respective photographers.

Front cover: Scott Turnmeyer (falcon); Wildlife Center of Virginia (people)

Back cover: Chad and Chris Saladin (falcon); Wildlife Center of Virginia (people). Spine: Scott Turnmeyer

Genesee Valley Audubon Society: 4, 7, 30 (hatch); Peter L. Gove: 32; Chad and Chris Saladin: 6, 8, 9, 10 (falcon), 12, 13, 14 (falcon), 30 (nest, lay, growing, head), 31 (flight, hunt); Shutterstock: 5 (crowd), 10 (background), 15 (crate), 21, 27 (feather); Scott Turnmeyer: 29; Lee Walker, Virginia Department of Game and Inland Fisheries: 31 (adult); Wildlife Center of Virginia: 5 (building), 15 (falcon), 16–20, 22–26, 27 (falcon)

Edited by Ryan Jacobson

Cover and book design by Jonathan Norberg

10 9 8 7 6 5 4 3 2 1
Copyright 2016 by Christie Gove-Berg
Published by Adventure Publications
820 Cleveland Street South
Cambridge, Minnesota 55008
1-800-678-7006
www.adventurepublications.net
All rights reserved
Printed in China
ISBN: 978-1-59193-516-2

Maggie
The One-Eyed Peregrine Falcon

A True Story of Rescue and Rehabilitation

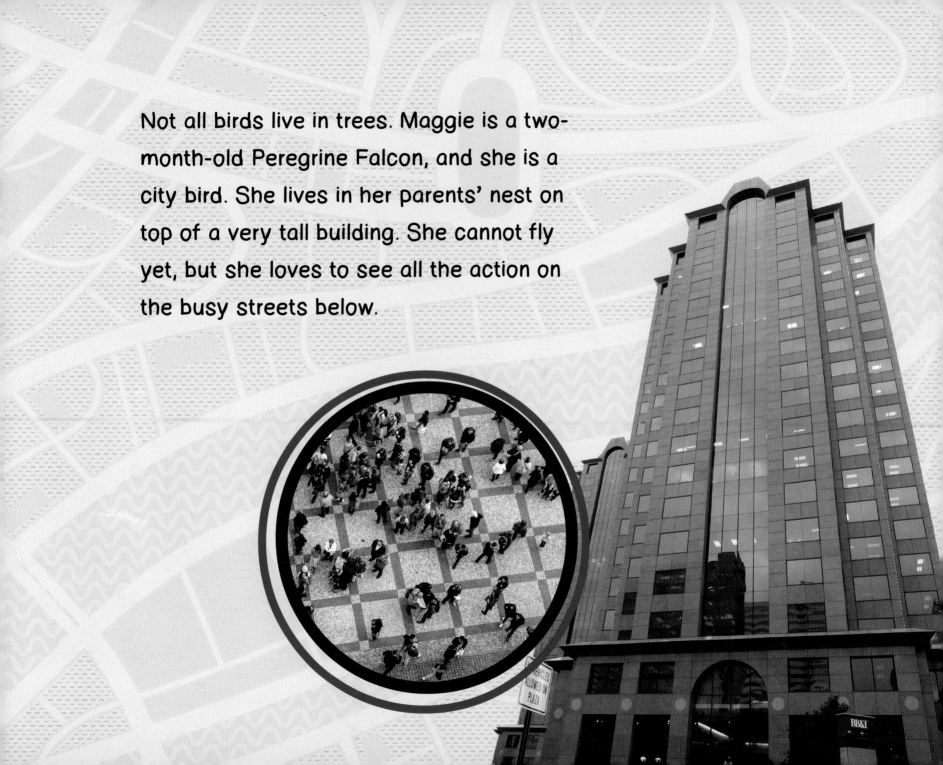

Not all birds live in trees. Maggie is a two-month-old Peregrine Falcon, and she is a city bird. She lives in her parents' nest on top of a very tall building. She cannot fly yet, but she loves to see all the action on the busy streets below.

Maggie watches her parents dive through the sky to catch food. Mostly, they hunt for pigeons. Sometimes, they get other birds, too. Maggie's parents bring the food to the nest for Maggie to eat. Yum!

With her tummy full, Maggie exercises. She takes little jumps along the ledge, while opening and closing her wings. When the wind blows under her, she lifts into the air. This feels right. Maggie is almost ready to fly.

The morning of her first flight is sunny but breezy. She moves to the edge of the nest and feels the push of the wind along her feathers.

Maggie opens her wings and leaps . . .

and flaps . . .

and flies!

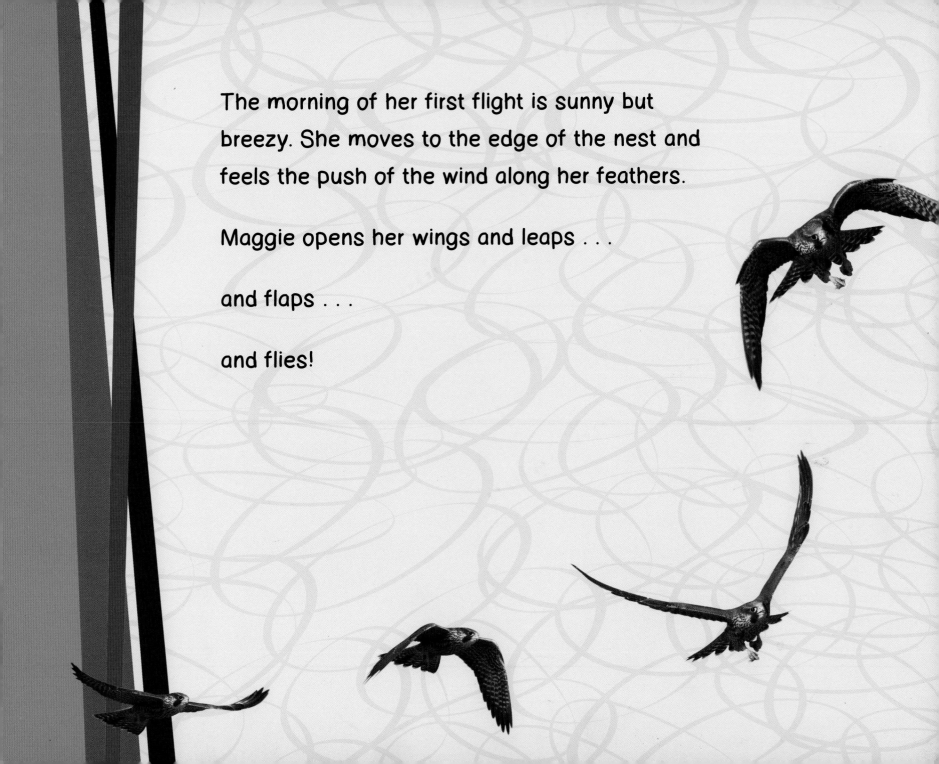

Her heart races. Sounds of the city swirl around her. She soars to the top of a construction crane and lands.

There, she watches smaller birds fly below. She dreams of catching her own food.

Two days go by. Maggie practices flying. She leaves the nest to explore. The sun warms her as she glides past buildings.

A strong wind lifts her. Maggie starts to turn, but she is pushed sideways by the breeze. Suddenly, in front of her, there is a building. It is close. Too close.

CRASH!

Maggie tumbles downward. She falls fast. She cannot stop.

And then she is on the ground. The pavement is hot. There are people everywhere. They lean in close.

Maggie realizes that her beak hurts. Her eyes aren't working right. What's wrong with her? Maggie cries out in fear and pain.

Special people come and pick her up. They seem to know what to do. She is put inside a crate and taken out of the city.

The people move her into a building. They call the place a wildlife hospital. They bring her to a quiet room and lift her from the crate.

Maggie shivers in fright. They shine a light in her eyes and stretch out her wings. They poke her with something sharp and take pictures of her. Maggie is too tired to fight. She lets them care for her.

Days pass, and the doctors keep checking on Maggie. She learns that her left eye was damaged when she hit the building. Plus, the tip of her beak broke off.

Luckily, the x-rays show that she didn't break any bones. And her beak will grow back, as good as new.

But the doctors are worried about her eye. If it doesn't get better, they will have to remove it. If they remove it, Maggie can never return to the wild.

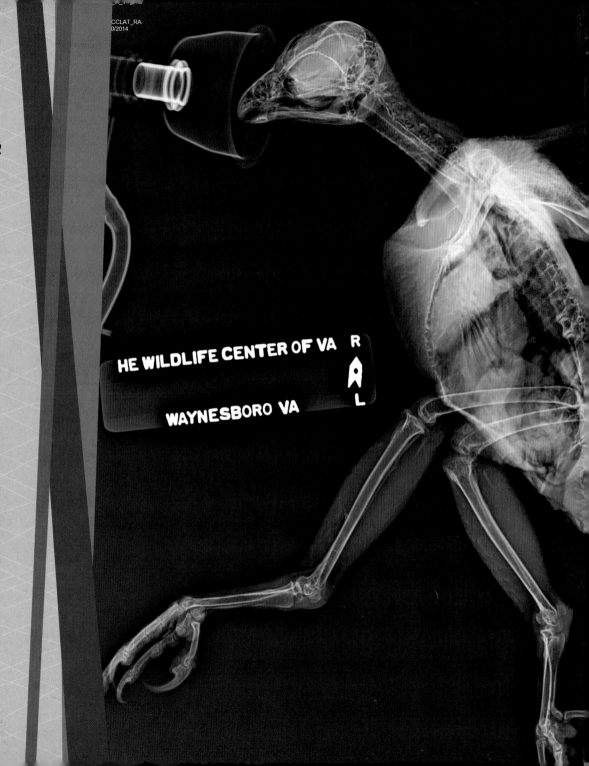

HE WILDLIFE CENTER OF VA

WAYNESBORO VA

R

A

L

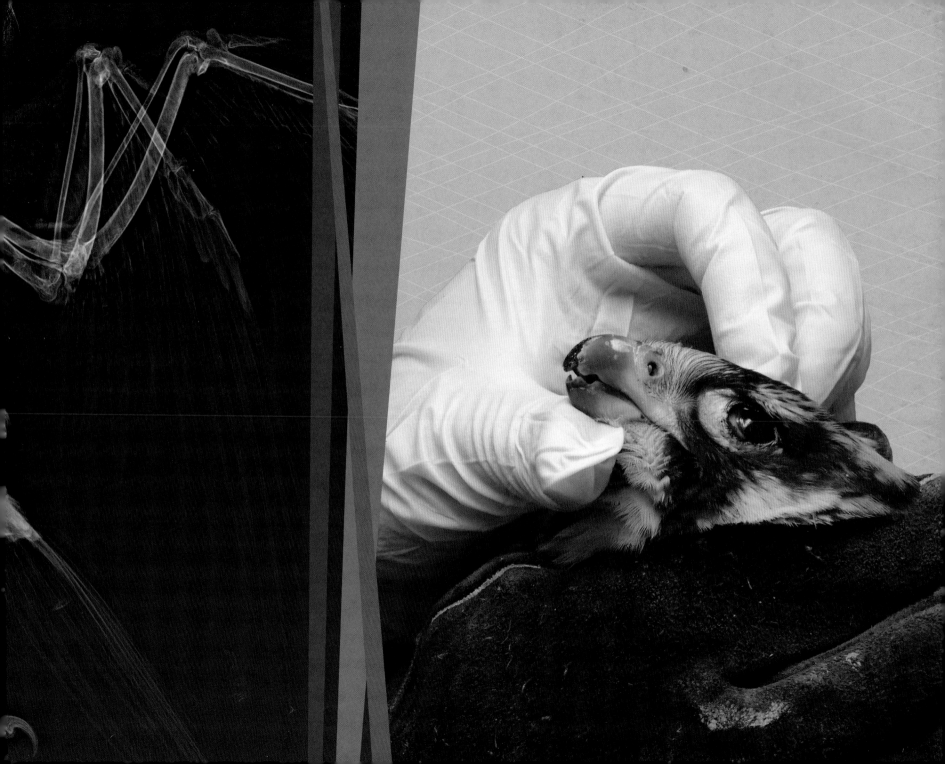

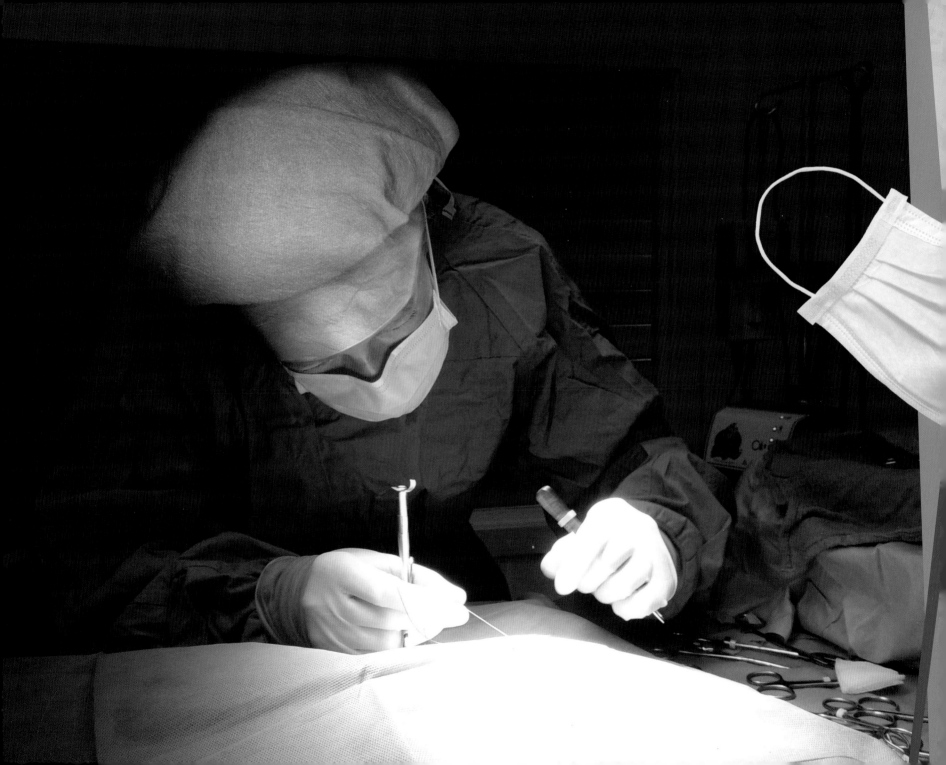

The doctors decide that the eye will never heal. They give Maggie medicine that makes her tired. Then, while Maggie is asleep, the doctors carefully remove the injured eye.

When Maggie wakes, there is less pain. She can see, but everything looks different.

Maggie is glad that the pain is gone, but she misses her parents' nest. She misses being outdoors. Outside feels much better than inside.

The people seem to notice her sadness. They move her to a large outdoor play area. The fresh air and warm sun feel good against her feathers. Maggie has a place to perch and space to fly.

A small bird gets into her play area, and Maggie feels hungry. She flies high into the air, then dives toward the bird. Down, down she comes, and . . . she misses it.

Now, Maggie understands. Without her left eye, she can't catch her own food. Peregrine Falcons need both eyes to hunt.

The people teach Maggie to sit on their arms. Their eyes are kind and their voices are soft. They reward her with tasty bites of food.

The people tell Maggie that she will be an education bird. She will live at the wildlife center, and she will teach children and adults about Peregrine Falcons.

This news makes Maggie happy. She has learned to like it there.

One day, Maggie is taken to meet a group of children. They are loud and wiggly, but they become quiet as soon as they see Maggie.

An adult tells the story of Maggie's life, and the children learn why Peregrine Falcons are important. They admire her feathers, her eye, and her talons. Maggie has become their teacher.

Thanks to Maggie, these children and their parents are learning to respect nature and, more importantly, to protect it. Maggie has become an education bird, and every day she will spread the word.

What are Peregrine Falcon families like?

Peregrine Falcons find their mates when they are one or two years old. They usually nest together for life, in or near the same area. They are known to be attentive, careful parents. Peregrine Falcons lay three or four eggs each year, in late March or early April. The male and female both incubate their eggs (sit on them to keep them warm), and both take turns hunting for food to share. Overall, the female does more of the incubating, while the male does more of the hunting. The eggs hatch about a month later.

It takes around six or seven weeks for young falcons to begin flying. Even after they learn to fly, the parents still bring them food until they can catch their own, about six weeks later.

Tell me more about Maggie and her family.

In 2002, Maggie's parents laid eggs in a nest box on the twenty-first floor of a building in Richmond, Virginia. The nest box was placed by wildlife biologists to encourage Peregrine Falcons to make their home there. Since then, this pair has produced dozens of chicks. Some of their chicks have been moved to other cities and national parks to help create self-sustaining areas where Peregrine Falcons live. The Virginia Department of Game and Inland Fisheries has worked hard to bring the story of Maggie's parents to the public, so people can learn more about Peregrine Falcons. People enjoy the department's live falcon cam, blog posts and a Fledge-watch when the falcons' chicks are about to fly. To learn more about the Richmond falcons, visit blog.wildlife.virginia.gov/falcon-cam.

As for Maggie, her story occurred in 2014, when she hit a building and injured her eye while learning to fly. She was rehabilitated at the Wildlife Center of Virginia. Due to her injury, she now lives at the Wildlife Center, helping to educate people about the recovery and management of Peregrine Falcons.

Why is Maggie named "Maggie"?

Maggie was given her name by Amanda Nicholson, Director of Outreach at the Wildlife Center of Virginia. Amanda chose the name "Maggie" to honor Maggie Lena Walker (July 15, 1864–December 15, 1934), an African-American businesswoman, teacher and an example for people with disabilities who lived in Richmond. Walker was the first female bank president to charter a bank in the U.S., and she wanted to make improvements in the way of life for women, especially African-American women.

choose a nest site   lay the eggs   eggs hatch in a month   growing up

Why did Maggie's parents raise their family in a busy city?

Wildlife biologists believe that Peregrine Falcons live up high because of how they hunt for food: They catch their prey by diving through the air. High places give the falcons a good view of prey birds. For this reason, Peregrine Falcons traditionally raise their chicks on cliff walls. The ledges of tall buildings also provide good places for falcons to nest; the numerous pigeons in big cities are a plentiful food source. That's part of the reason why Maggie's parents chose to live there.

Sometimes, wildlife biologists, private peregrine conservation groups and raptor centers bring young Peregrine Falcons into big cities (and into certain natural areas) on purpose. This is called "hacking." The hope behind this method is that the falcons will return as adults and build their own nests there. Hacking gives falcons more places to live, which increases their population. Maggie's parents were hacked in Richmond, Virginia, another reason they chose to nest in the city.

Where else do Peregrine Falcons live?

Peregrine Falcons are among the most widespread birds in the world. They are found on all continents, except Antarctica, and they can be seen in all 50 U.S. states. Some Peregrine Falcons migrate—or fly south for winter—and some don't. Those that nest in fairly cold climates often migrate in order to find enough food during winter. (Peregrine actually means "wanderer" or "pilgrim" because those that migrate will cover thousands of miles on their journey.) Falcons that nest in warmer climates often don't migrate because food is available year-round.

How do Peregrine Falcons catch their food?

The Peregrine Falcon is the fastest animal on the planet. It can reach speeds of more than 200 miles per hour. Peregrine Falcons use that speed to hunt other birds. The falcons fly high in the sky, and when they spot their prey, they put their wings straight back and dive downward. This dive is called a "stoop." It begins as high as 3,000 feet above the prey. The falcons strike their prey feet first. Then they loop through the air to grab the prey as it falls.

baby peregrine falcon

first flight at 6 weeks

learn to hunt

mature adult: 1–2 years

Why were Peregrine Falcons on the Endangered Species List?

A chemical called DDT was commonly used in farming from the 1940s to 1960s. Small birds fed on DDT-covered grains and seeds from farm fields. Peregrine Falcons ate those small birds, and the DDT affected them. After many years, people realized that DDT was thinning the eggshells of raptors, like Peregrine Falcons and Bald Eagles. The parents sat on the eggs to incubate them, and thin shells caused the eggs to crack before the chicks were ready to hatch. The chicks could not survive.

For a time, Peregrine Falcons nearly disappeared. But since the removal of DDT from the environment, Peregrine Falcons have done very well. They were taken off the Endangered Species List in 1999, but they're still monitored by raptor and environmental groups.

How can I learn more about Peregrine Falcons?

Consider watching a webcam of a falcon family. There are many falcon cams available online, such as raptorresource.org, peregrinefund.org, rfalconcam.com/rfc-main and blog.wildlife.virginia.gov/falcon-cam.

Tell me more about wildlife hospitals.

Wildlife hospitals strive to care for wild birds, mammals, reptiles and amphibians. Their goal is to treat and return to the wild all the creatures that are brought to them. Maggie's story was told in collaboration with the Wildlife Center of Virginia, a wildlife hospital with a mission of teaching the world to care about animals and the environment. The Wildlife Center shares the stories of its animals to illustrate the wider problems that wildlife face—litter, pesticides, free-roaming domestic animals, habitat loss and diseases—and challenges people of all ages to take action to protect wildlife.

Most raptor centers and wildlife hospitals are non-profit and depend mainly on donations to do their work. So if you value their contributions to our natural world, consider giving them a financial donation. By buying this book, you are supporting the Wildlife Center of Virginia.

About the Author

Christie Gove-Berg loves nature and wildlife. Her first book, *Esther the Eaglet: A True Story of Rescue and Rehabilitation*, was written after an injured eaglet was rescued on her parents' land. This second story was inspired by Maggie, a young Peregrine Falcon who was injured while learning to fly. Maggie is now an education bird at the Wildlife Center of Virginia. A portion of the profits from each book sold will go to the Wildlife Center of Virginia.

Christie has written three children's books. She spends her free time with her family.